Conten

Welcome To GUIDELINE

These pages will help you enjoy the journey on the North Yorkshire Moors Railway. The first half of the book can be used from either Pickering or Grosmont and describes the lineside features which make this journey one of the finest in the country.

Pages 12 to 25 give more detail about the railway, its history and its surroundings. They are best read before or after your journey, but not on the train — there's too much to see through the windows!

A JOURNEY ACROSS TIME

The lineside features change with every curve of the track. They reflect thousands of years of man's activities and millions of years of nature's action.

See 3,000-year-old defensive works of Bronze Age man and a couple of minutes later glimpse twentieth century defences at Fylingdales where, since 1964, the famous 'Golf Balls' and now a huge Pyramid have kept vigil for unwelcome missiles.

Lineside cottages and castles — even the stations themselves — have been the subjects of artists' brushes and television dramas. The landscapes of the National Park through which the line passes are truly spectacular: for almost all of the 18 miles the train takes you through Sites of Special Scientific Interest — places of national importance because of their unique natural history. Patience will be rewarded by the sight of rare birds, animals and flowers.

On a different scale, the train is dwarfed by the cliffs of the Newtondale Gorge. Carved at the end of the ice age by millions of gallons of water, it's Britain's answer to the Grand Canyon.

Man-made and natural wonders abound: the railway is the thread which links all these gems together.

6619 at Thomason Foss

GROSMONT STATION

TUNNEL

Stephenson's Original Trackbed

GOATHLAND

NEWTONDALE HALT

LEVISHAM STATION

PICKERING STATION

N

A WORD OF WARNING

Don't expect to see it all on one journey. Regular travellers will explain that not only does the scenery change dramatically with the seasons, but at different times of the day you may notice different birds and animals. So take your time, after all, the North York Moors National Park was set aside because of its peace and beauty.

Perhaps the best way of really getting to know the area is by breaking your journey at one of the stations and exploring on foot. There are easy walks (and longer ones) which have been devised especially to help you understand more about this very special place.

ALL ABOARD

Over 150 years ago this railway became George Stephenson's biggest challenge. His navvies worked against all the odds to create the line. Rivers and waterfalls, steep hills and bogs — nothing was allowed to hinder the railway's progress. The line weaves together a triumph of the railway

45428 Eric Treacy in Newtondale

age and the beauty of the National Park with its forests, farmland, moors and picture-postcard hamlets.

So sit back and prepare for one of Britain's best railway journeys.

The Journey

1 PICKERING TO LEVISHAM

LEVISHAM STATION

Pickering Castle

The arches of **lime kilns** can be seen to the west of the line. Limestone was needed to fertilise the fields further north and the supply at Pickering was a key reason why the line was built. Limestone is still quarried a little further along the line near New Bridge.

FARWATH

NEW BRIDGE

PICKERING STATION

Pickering Castle stands high on the hill overlooking the station. Originally built by the Normans as a timber fort, it was rebuilt following fourteenth century raids by Scotland's Robert the Bruce. Almost every king of medieval England stayed here, most to enjoy the hunt in nearby Blansby Park, but some as prisoner.

The **Trout Farm** is home to 1½ million young trout which are raised here, destined for the dinner table, or for re-stocking rivers throughout the country. Visitors who try their hand with a rod and line are almost guaranteed a catch.

The **level crossing** at New Bridge marks the boundary of the North York Moors National Park. Although called a National Park, this spectacular countryside is a living, working landscape and still privately owned by farmers and landowners. Every visitor is asked to show good countryside manners and join those who live and work here in protecting this precious resource for future generations.

New Bridge level crossing

Levisham

Blansby Park was a more traditional park — a place of sport and hunting for kings. By 1600 the Park had been extended with a ditch and palisade running almost along the line of the present track. 600 fallow deer browsed the woodland here and even today you may spot deer, especially further up the line between Levisham and Fen Bog. Much of the land around here has remained in Royal hands since the Norman conquest and the Queen still holds this land as part of the Duchy of Lancaster.

Farwath cottages are typical railway cottages of the last century. In the past special market-day trains stopped here and at other isolated cottages to take goods or shoppers to Pickering market. In more recent years, trains have provided an emergency service when snow has blocked the difficult roads and tracks in this part of the Moors.

Levisham Station may remind you of films or television series you have seen. Amongst its many starring roles, it was the Melton Carbury of Brideshead Revisited, and featured in Poirot, Sherlock Holmes, All Creatures Great and Small. Look at the slate roofs and overhanging eaves of the station buildings which are typical of those along the line. Until the coming of the railway, the farms and cottages of Newtondale were thatched or sometimes roofed with red clay pantiles made just south of Pickering. Railway cottages and station buildings along the line were the first to use slate. Its transport from North Wales or the Lake District was made possible by the railways.

Levisham village lies out of sight some 1½ miles (2.4km) south east of the station. The distance, added to a climb of 300 feet (90m) from the valley floor, made the station somewhat inconvenient for the village. But station staff would fend off angry travellers by saying that the station would look silly in the village if the railway line was in the valley! Today's station staff are far more helpful and can direct you to some of the spectacular walks around Newtondale.

2 LEVISHAM TO NEWTONDALE HALT

RAINDALE

NEWTONDALE HALT

SKELTON TOWER

LEVISHAM STATION

The Grange was once the Raindale New Inn. When the railway opened in 1836 it was a useful place to pause and have a drink on the 2 hour journey between Pickering and Grosmont. For the first nine years, the railway relied on horses to pull the carriages and it was here that a new pair of horses was put into the harness to haul the train up to the summit.

On the down hill trip to Pickering, the horses had an easier time. They were unhitched and put in a 'dandy cart' behind the carriage and the train freewheeled down towards Pickering, with the horses no doubt enjoying the rest and the passengers hoping that the brakeman had his wits about him!

The principle of putting the horse in a cart behind the carriages was first proposed by Stephenson 10 years earlier and, by giving the horses a rest, increased the amount of work they could do each day.

Raindale Water Mill stood here. Its fourteen foot (4.25m) waterwheel providing the power to grind local-grown wheat into flour. In 1915, the stream changed course and the mill was forced to stop. The entire mill was later removed to the Castle Museum in York where it can now be seen once again milling flour.

Raindale Watermill

The Grange

Skelton Tower sits on the edge of the cliff overlooking the line and looking like the ruin of some ancient castle keep. But it was in Victorian times that Robert Skelton, the vicar of Levisham, built the two-storeyed tower. Some say he wrote his sermons here, others imply he escaped here for a quiet drink!

An ironstone mine was opened here in 1857. A 240 foot (73m) shaft was sunk but the mine was unprofitable and closed. Local connections with an iron industry go back much further. There was a forge in Levisham in 1207 and two medieval iron smelting sites are close to the railway in Newtondale. Whilst high on the moors above the line is the site of unique 'bloomery' where the earliest industrial revolution must have taken place during the Iron Age, over two thousand years ago.

The **forests** of Newtondale are new. In 1929 the hillsides were bare, open sheep pasture when the first Spruce and Fir trees were planted here as part of a national campaign to make Britian self-sufficient in timber production. Much of this first crop has now been felled, the trunks of many of the huge Douglas Firs weighing over a tonne. As part of the Forestry Commission's plans for Newtondale, great emphasis is now placed on conservation. Different types of trees are planted and near the railway several wildlife areas have been created.

Newtondale Well lies just below the cliffs and was once famed for its mineral waters. The trace of buildings and large stone tanks are all that can be seen today, but 300 years ago many people came here to take the waters. On Midsummer's Day young people came to join in what their elders considered to be somewhat dubious festivities. Last century the potential of the mineral waters was considered so great that a large area of Newtondale was offered for sale with the ideal that it be developed as an inland spa to rival Buxton and Harrogate.

80135 Newtondale Halt

Newtondale Halt was opened in 1981 to enable visitors to explore this remote part of Newtondale. It was a joint project involving the Railway, the National Park Authority, the Countryside Commission and the Forestry Commision. A series of waymarked walks and paths go through the forest, some leading to spectacular viewpoints from the high cliffs.

Newtondale Halt

3 NEWTONDALE HALT TO GOATHLAND

The cliffs which tower above the valley are formed of Kellaways Rock, a sandstone laid down 150 million years ago when the area was covered by a shallow sea. You can still see the thin, alternating layers of sand laid down by tides all those years ago. The 400 feet (120m) deep Newtondale Gorge was carved relatively recently. A mere 10,000 years ago, melting ice started to trickle, then to flow, and finally a torrent of millions of gallons of water carved this natural wonder during a period of perhaps ten or twenty years.

Killing Nab Scar

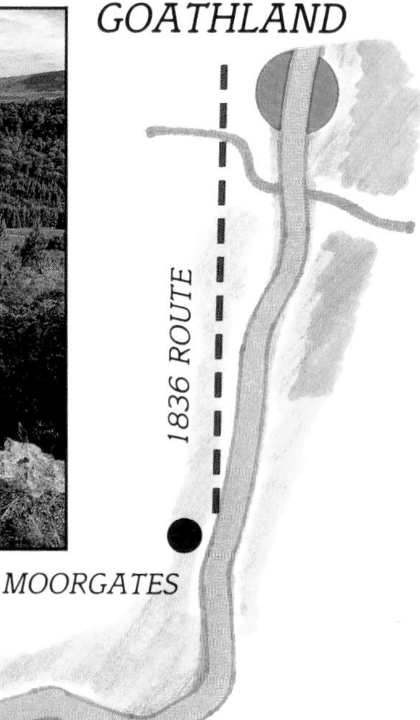

Killing Nab Scar was the breeding ground of peregrine falcons in 1612 when the inhabitants of Goathland were ordered to look after them 'for the King's Use.' Today, the plantations are the breeding ground of sparrowhawks who hunt along the rides and clearings in the forest. Other birds of prey may be seen further along the dale — including the very rare merlin.

10,000 years ago these **moors** were covered in natural forest. Early man cleared and burned areas to provide grazing for wild and domestic animals. Today the moors are managed in more or less the same way: controlled burning helps the growth of young heather shoots on which sheep and grouse feed. The small burnt areas (or

The Cliffs

'swiddens') provide a patchwork of young and old heather making ideal nesting conditions for red grouse and other wild birds.

Fen Bog Nature Reserve still has a remnant of the dense woodland which flourished here 10,000 years ago. It was mainly birch, alder and willow. 5,000 years ago much of the woodland began to die out and it was replaced by the reedswamp still to be seen in the drainage channels. Today Fen Bog is a unique mixture of bog and fenland plants and is noted for its dragonflies and many bird species. Fen Bog is over 38 feet (11.8m) deep and was one of the major difficulties Stephenson had to face when building the railway. His navvies sank brushwood, timber and even sheep fleeces filled with heather to produce a causeway on which to lay the track. By 1859 these foundations had rotted and the long hot summer caused the rails to buckle. On Saturday, 8th August, an engine and two carriages plunged into the bog, with the train crew gallantly rescuing all the passengers from a sticky end.

Summit is about 550 feet (160m) above sea level and in the next 5½ miles the line drops almost 500 feet (150m) to the Esk Valley at Grosmont.

Moorgates marks the point where Stephenson's original 1836 route diverges from the present line. To the west you will see the embankment, the gate-keeper's cottage and the 'Cattle Arch'. This bridge was built to let cattle move freely between the coast and the Plain of York, some 25 miles to the west: before the coming of the railway, there was neither fence nor wall to restrict such movement over the moors.

Abbot's House is the site where monks settled in about 1100, and it marks the first records of Goathland. Henry I allowed the monks the privilege of cutting timber from his Forest of Pickering for their buildings and fences on condition that they should provide food and a bed for any poor travellers who passed their door.

Goathland Station has barely changed since it was opened on 1st July, 1865. Its design was identical to dozens of other North Eastern Railway stations of that period, including several on the Esk Valley line between Whitby and Middlesbrough.

Goathland Station

4 GOATHLAND TO GROSMONT

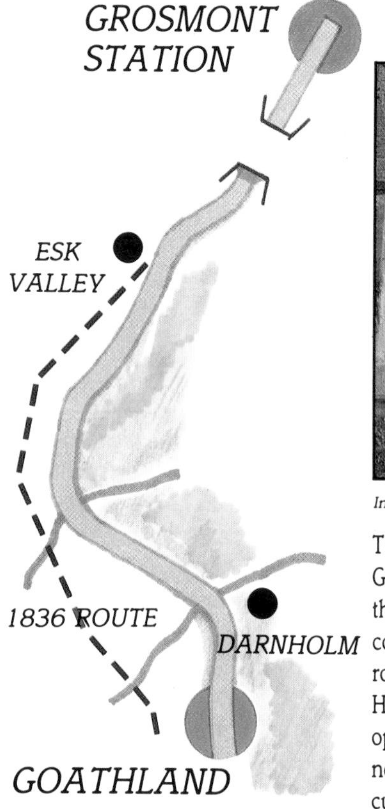

Incline Cottage, Beck Hole

The **1 in 49 gradient** between Goathland and Grosmont is one of the steepest rail gradients in the country. It replaced the 1 in 10 rope-worked incline between Beck Hole and Goathland which operated from 1836 to 1865. The new route involved blasting a cutting through the rocks. Rock falls were so frequent that a watchman patrolled the line each night and walked the line between Esk Valley and Goathland Station each morning before the arrival of the 6 a.m. mail train from York. These safety patrols continued every day for over 50 years until grass and scrub stabilised the banks.

Approaching Esk Valley Cottages

Darnholm was the 'dark meadow' whilst further down the valley was 'Sommerholm' — the meadow grazed in summertime. There was a fulling mill at Darnholm where cloth was spread in the tenter field to be bleached by the sun, but this was before the coming of the railway with its smoke and soot!

The **Murk Esk** river is crossed four times in half a mile and there is an almost sheer drop of 100 feet (30m) to the valley floor. The hamlet of Beck Hole, a popular spot for visitors during Victorian and Edwardian times, lies in the valley below.

Esk Valley once supplied the labour force for the nearby ironstone mines. Before the terrace of 24 cottages was built in 1870, there was a unique complex for key workers with living accommodation on the first floor and blacksmith's shop, joiner's, the mine office and a wash house on the lower level. For 100 years the villagers relied entirely on the railway. Food, fuel and everyday necessities were delivered fortnightly by rail. It was only when the villagers raised the cash amongst themselves that a road was built to the village in October 1951.

The **1836 route,** to the north of the line, provides one of the most popular walks in the National Park — the Historical Rail Trail. Beyond the track, in the fields can be seen the remains of railway sidings, mine shafts and the gunpowder store — all that remains of the Esk Valley Ironstone Mines of 1860-1875.

Engine sheds are relatively new to Grosmont. In earlier time repairs and maintenance could be carried out at convenient depots anywhere on the rail network. It was only when the line was re-opened by the Railway Trust in the 1970s that there was need for all the workshop and storage facilities of an operational railway to be located here. Visitors can walk to the sheds from Grosmont Station and see many of the activities required to keep the trains running.

Grosmont (pronounced 'Grow-mont') takes its name from 'Grandimont', the name of the mother church from where monks came to found a priory near here in 1204. Other than tiny traces of earthworks, nothing remains of the priory. The present village owes its existence to the railway. When Stephenson planned his route in the 1830s, he used the Murk Esk valley as his route southwards. But he had to build a tunnel through Lease Rigg and in so doing accidentally discovered rich deposits of iron. By 1836 the Tunnel Inn, a few cottages, workshops and a warehouse had been erected. This cluster of buildings was known simply as Tunnel. As the ironstone was mined, the population grew. By the 1870s it was over 1,500 and the village had become known as Grosmont. In addition to blast furnaces, there were brick works, lime kilns, stone quarries and whinstone mines: a bustling industrial community with smoke and fumes billowing from chimneys, the roar of furnaces day and night, and the whistling and clanking of trains as they shunted along the many sidings. Today the community is smaller, but it still has a love-hate relationship with the railway which gave birth to it.

Grosmont Station

Lineside Wonders

1 NATURE'S LINESIDE WONDERS

Although the lineside is exceptionally rich in wildlife, much of it may be hard to spot from the carriage window. Flowers and fungi may be too small to see, and many birds and animals flee from the noise of the train. A short walk from any station will help you discover the sights, sounds and smells of the countryside at first hand.

Nevertheless, on many journeys travellers can watch nature unfolding before them: perhaps an ungainly heron taking off as if in slow motion, and then flying alongside the train; or roe deer browsing in a forest clearing.

In May and June the boggy land around Fen Bog is white with cotton grass, whose fine, white, hairy seed pods carry the fruit long distances on the wind.

From June to August the ditches and embankments around Levisham are creamy-white with the sweet-smelling flowers of meadowsweet. In medieval times they were spread amongst the rushes on the floors of cottages to disguise the smells.

Another fragrant plant of damp patches is the Bog Myrtle which was used to make Gale Beer, a popular and thirst-quenching drink for the navvies when building the railway.

In the late summer the glory of the moors is heather — mile upon mile of purple flowers forming the largest single area of heather moorland in England. In early spring or autumn, small patches of heather are burned to encourage new growth. But when accidental fire is started, the results can be disastrous with huge areas of moorland never fully recovering.

The Moors with Fylingdales Early Warning Station

Although bracken provides a great splash of golden colour in autumn, it is an unwelcome intruder. Descended from ferns which thrived here 300 million years ago, today the fast-growing bracken is threatening to take over much of the heather moorland. As well as stifling the heather — and thus the use of the moors by grouse and sheep — bracken can be poisonous to cattle and spreads disease in sheep. The National Park Authority and landowners are working together to keep bracken in check before it changes the landscape of the Park forever.

The lapwing is perhaps the best known moorland bird. Its twisting flight shows a flash of black and white. The curlew's 5 inch (125mm) curved bill makes it an easily recognised bird. It probes damp earth and water searching out worms and insects. Of the falcons of the moors the kestrel is the most common, feeding on small mammals. The rare merlin is also found on the moors, it swoops and spirals in pursuit of smaller birds such as meadow pippits.

Adders often bask on rocks or railway sleepers in the warm sun. Up to two feet (60cm) long, they are Britain's only poisonous snake. They kill their prey (usually mice and voles) with the powerful venom from their upper fangs. However the adder is not harmful to man if left alone.

FOREST

For 2,000 years native trees provided all that we wanted for building, fuel and a thousand other things. But slowly over the years the country became reliant on imports and the German U-Boat blockade of the First World War finally brought things to a head. In 1919 the Forestry Commission was established to make the country self-sufficient in timber.

Almost immediately, land was purchased near here and the first trees were planted in 1921. Many of these early trees have now reached maturity and are being felled. When the land is replanted the foresters of today pay more attention to landscape, recreation and wildlife conservation.

Around Newtondale Halt are ponds and areas laid out to encourage wildlife, and there are fine walks from which to discover the secrets of the forest.

The trees of Newtondale include Sitka and Norway Spruce, Japanese Larch, Douglas Fir and Scots Pine. More native trees are also being planted to increase the wildlife interest of the area.

Newtondale Forest

GEOLOGY IN ACTION

Rocks form the foundation for the shape of the land, dictating the location of villages and towns, farming and wildlife. Products of local rocks were a key reason for the building of the railway and have been exploited all along the line — iron, alum, lime, road materials, building stone and even coal.

Imagine that the rocks form a giant layer cake which has tilted and then had parts of its top layers removed. The railway takes us on a geological journey slicing through this layer cake.

ONE

180 million years ago the whole area lay beneath a shallow sea. Gradually, over thousands of years, fine silt and mud fell to the ocean floor and was compressed to form a rock called the Lias. Also squashed in the mud were many small sea creatures whose fossilised remains are found today. Iron-rich deposits were laid on top forming the rocks which were mined around Grosmont, and gave birth to the Cleveland Iron Industry.

In swampy areas, trees like the giant Monkey Puzzle grew. These fell to the seafloor and were compressed to form jet, a hard black mineral which can be carved into jewellery made especially fashionable by Queen Victoria.

TWO

As the sea became shallower, the area was covered by the delta of a huge river. Layers of sand and silt washed down this river were compressed to form sandstone. Local buildings were made of this stone and huge quantities were transported throughout the country by rail. London's streets were paved, not with gold, but with stone from the North York Moors.

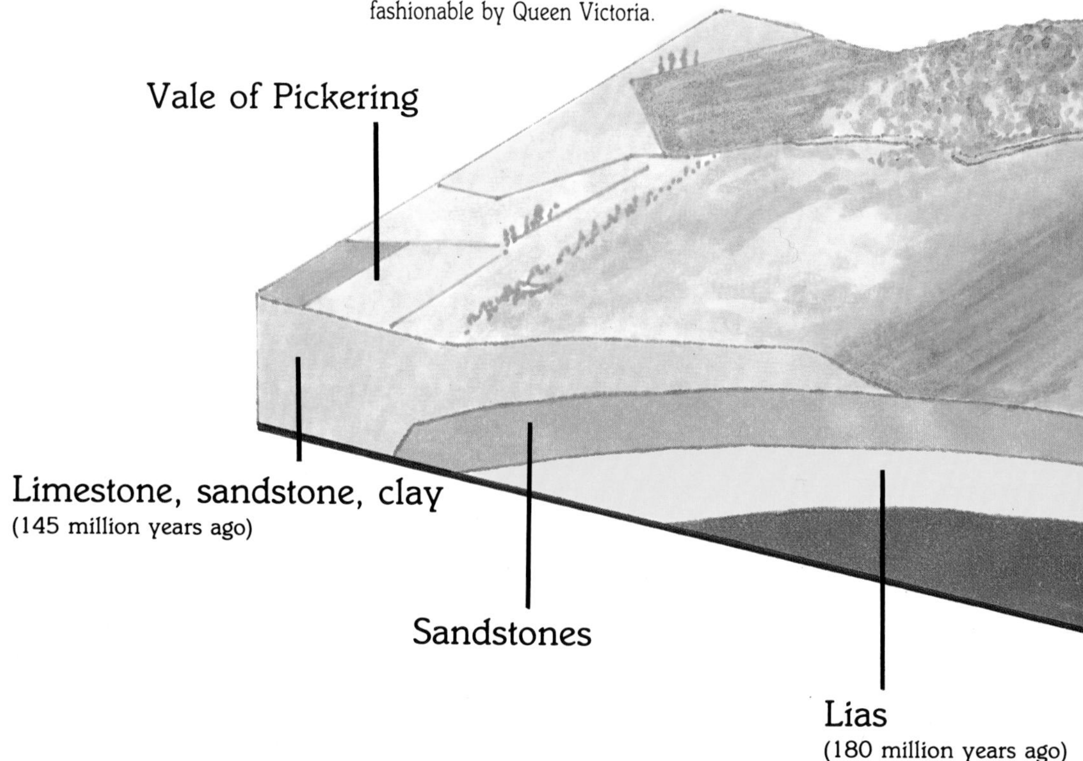

THREE

A few million years later the sea once again engulfed the area and in the resulting warm, shallow sea more sand and tiny creatures were deposited and compressed to form limestone which is quarried at New Bridge near Pickering. The top of our layer cake is made of dark coloured Kimmeridge Clay. Most of this has been eroded but a blob of this 'icing' has withstood frost, rain and wind remaining as a rounded hill to the west of the line at Pickering.

FOUR

Whilst this layering was taking place, other forces folded, twisted and tilted the rocks. About 58 million years ago and 1,000 miles (1,600 km) away a group of rocks were being pushed upwards to form the Alps. Tensions in the earth's crust caused great cracks or 'faults' to form and into one of these, molten rock rushed up to the surface. When it cooled, this hard, volcanic rock formed a great scar, not only across the moors but as far as Scotland. This 'whinstone' has been quarried and mined around Goathland for crushing into roadstone or cutting into setts for the streets of many towns and cities.

FIVE

The last major shaping of the land took place at the end of the Ice Age. Huge lakes formed where water was trapped by solid walls of ice and one such lake in Eskdale eventually overflowed. 2½ billion gallons (11 billion litres) rushed into what was a small valley and over just a few years the icy torrent cut a 400 feet (120m) gorge, 14 miles (22 km) long — the Newtondale Gorge.

The story continues: every shower of rain, every frosty morning makes its mark on the landscape. But our concern is for a far shorter period than the millions of years which shaped this spectacular area.

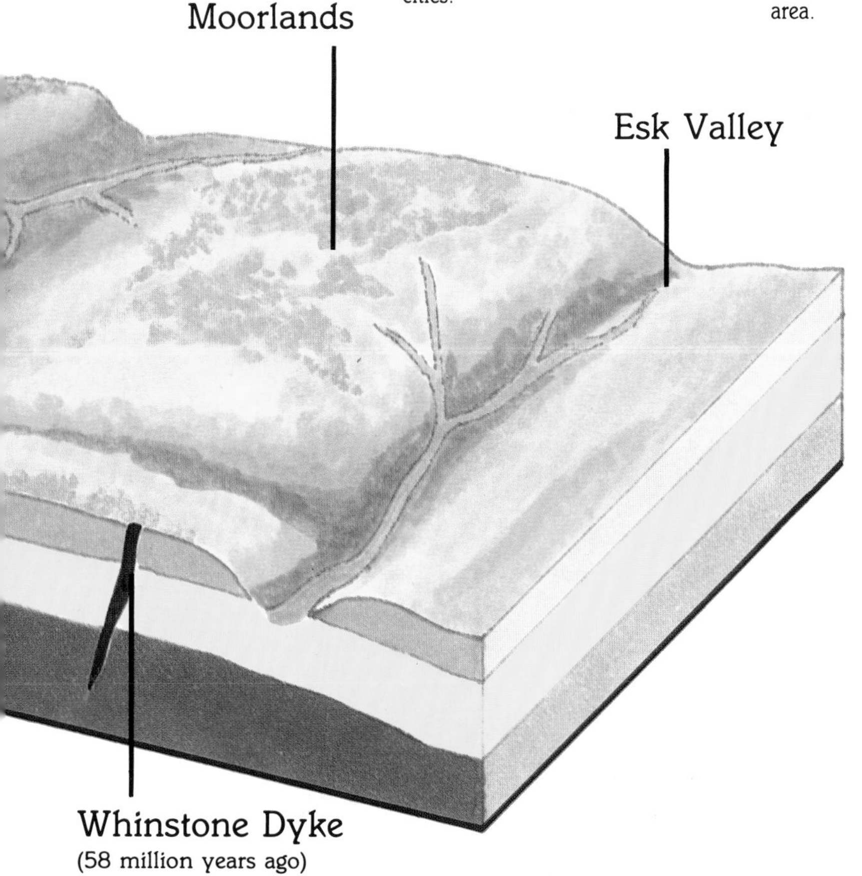

Railway History

1 PLANNING THE ROUTE

A couple of hundred years ago, people said that there was only one road to Whitby: the sea. Moorland roads were often impassable and in the eighteenth century the journey was considered so perilous that intending travellers would make out a will before venturing over the moors.

In 1793 a canal was planned between Whitby and Pickering. It was estimated that 100 locks would be needed in the first eight miles, so the consequent cost put it out of the running.

Traders in Whitby were desperate. The shipbuilding industry was in decline. Alum works were closing. Fewer whalers were using the docks which were in any case, silting up. It was a case of recession which Whitby businessmen resolved to fight.

A canal had proved impracticable so rail was considered the only answer. Two rival routes from Whitby were advocated: one along the Esk Valley to Middlesbrough and one cutting across the moors to Pickering. Both were surveyed and at a meeting in 1831 it was agreed to ask George Stephenson to look more closely at the Pickering option. He concluded that an inexpensive, horse-drawn railway would meet local needs at a price which backers could afford.

Stephenson suggested a route from Whitby, along the Esk Valley and then southwards. He planned a 1½ mile (2.4 km) tunnel beneath the moors from Hunt House near Goathland to the top of Newtondale and sank a 193 foot (60m) borehole to test the rock, but mindful of the limited budget, he decided on another route which incorporated a mile long (1.6 km) incline between Beck Hole and Goathland.

George Stephenson

2 THE MEN WHO BUILT THE RAILWAY

Work started in September, 1833 with an army of navvies descending on the route with their picks, shovels and wheel barrows. They diverted streams and rivers, built dozens of timber bridges and blasted a 120 yard (110m) tunnel 14 feet high by 10 feet wide (4m x 3m) through the rock at Grosmont.

By 1835 the route was complete from Whitby to the new tunnel, a distance of over 6 miles (10 km). This section was pressed into service and in the first year carried 10,000 tons of stone from Grosmont to Whitby. By May 15th the Railway's Directors had enough confidence to make a trip from Whitby to Grosmont in the first class coach 'Premier' and three weeks later, on June 8th a regular passenger service started over this section of the line, carrying 6,000 passengers in the first three months.

Fares were one shilling outside (sitting on the roof of the coach) and one shilling and three pence inside. On July 18th, a six penny ticket was available for use in the second class coach, and at the other end of the line, passengers were carried over the section of track which had been completed between Pickering and Raindale.

But whilst the great and good were enjoying the novelty of the journey, the navvies were still facing the two toughest sections of the railway: the steep incline between Beck Hole and Goathland, and the dreaded Fen Bog, deep, sticky, remote and, for much of the year, cold and inhospitable.

Throughout the winter the attempt to tame Fen Bog continued. Carter's House was pressed into service as shelter, alehouse and payroom and in the small, smokey room, engineers discussed how to make a stable track for the railway.

An ingenious combination of timber, heather, brushwood and sheep's fleeces finally created a causeway over the bog. At the same time, work on the rope-worked Beck Hole incline was completed. Stephenson and his colleagues were well pleased — and probably not a little relieved.

With brass bands, bunting and brave speeches the complete route was opened on 26th May, 1836. Thousands turned out to cheer this miracle of modern engineering: a horse pulling a coach at ten miles per hour (16 kph) on a track which stretched from Whitby to Pickering. The line instantly became one of the north's great wonders.

80135 passing Fen Bog

3 WORLD'S FIRST RAILWAY EXCURSIONS

The world's first cheap day excursion trains were run here on August 7th and 8th, 1839. A bazaar was being held to raise money to build a church for the blossoming village of Grosmont and the railway company advertised an hourly service from Whitby, with the first departure at 5 a.m. A year later, special trains were running again, this time for the foundation stone laying ceremony! (The church was opened in 1842, but the phenomenal growth of Grosmont needed an even bigger church by 1875).

Grosmont

4 GETTING ALL STEAMED UP

All this traffic was hauled by horses: one horse per coach. And it took 2½ hours to get from Whitby to Pickering. Not very economic; not very fast.

"One engine is worth 50 horses", said Stephenson. Elsewhere, steam locomotives were proving their worth and when the line was bought by George Hudson's York and North Midland Railway, the isolated horse-drawn railway was transformed.

Tunnel Inn (line drawings reproduced from a painting in Whitby Museum)

A new tunnel was built at Grosmont and new bridges constructed; permanent station buildings were erected at Whitby, Grosmont, Goathland and Pickering; sharp curves were straightened out, or short lengths of new line laid to by-pass the most difficult sections; engine sheds were constructed at the foot of the Beck Hole incline to serve the section between the incline and Whitby; and a new heavier track was laid.

The age of steam had arrived, yet despite the investment of Hudson, there was still a major obstacle to efficient through trains: the Beck Hole Incline was out of place on a 'modern' railway.

5 THE BECK HOLE INCLINE

When the line first opened, the incline was worked by gravity. A 6 inch (150mm) rope was fixed to the carriage to be hauled up, the rope passed round a ten foot (3m) wooden drum at Incline Top and the other end was fastened to a 4-ton water tank on wheels. The weight of the full tank travelling down the slope pulled the carriage to the top, the water from the tank was emptied into the Murk Esk and a nearby farmer brought his horses to haul the empty tank back to the top ready for the next journey.

The rope often became snagged, or was run over by the coach wheels and damaged. It was replaced with wire and the water tank and drum gave way to a stationary steam engine, but the incline still proved an irritating and dangerous feature of the line. Several times the wire snapped sending waggons careering down into Beck Hole. On one occasion a train load of herrings was derailed, leaving a nasty stench hanging over the place for weeks.

On the frosty evening of February 10th, 1864, the worst accident happened. Despite valiant efforts by the guard, the last passenger train of the day ran away down the incline and overturned at the bottom. Two passengers were killed and 13 injured.

The railway company was quick to respond and a little over a year later a new route was opened which by-passed the incline.

Beck Hole

6 SIGNALS AND STATIONS

In the early days of the line, signals were given by flags: White — 'go on'; Red — 'go slow'; Blue — 'stop'. Other types of signals were tried elsewhere, including rotating boards and discs, before the traditional 'semaphore' signal was developed in the 1840s.

To avoid accidents on single lines a 'block working' system was introduced. A ticket, staff or tablet was handed to the driver and no other train would then be allowed on that section of line until the token was handed back to the signalman.

The invention of the electric telegraph meant that signal boxes could communicate with each other, and key tokens could be issued by instruments at each box. This saved waiting for a train in the other direction to return the token to the issuing box, or for someone to walk between the two boxes.

Once there were eight signal boxes on the line at Grosmont, Deviation Junction, Goathland, Summit, Newtondale, Levisham, Farwath, New Bridge and Pickering. Today there are boxes at Grosmont, Goathland, Levisham and New Bridge.

STATIONS

There were stations at Whitby and Pickering before there were any mainline terminii in London. Amongst railway buildings from the 1830s look at Grosmont (Post Office and Inn), at Goathland (various buildings on the original route between Beck Hole and Moorgates) and at Levisham.

The present day stations at Grosmont and Pickering date from the coming of steam in 1845, whilst Goathland Station is the baby of the family being a mere 130 years old!

7 A NEW TICKET

For almost 130 years the railway fulfilled its promise of linking Whitby to the outside world. But in the 1960s the line was declared uneconomic and, with hundreds of miles elsewhere, it was closed.

For many of the severed branch lines this was the end of an era. However a group of local people met in 1967 with the aim of re-opening the line to passenger traffic. By an amazing combination of persuasive talking, successful fund-raising and thousands of hours of back-breaking work, the railway was officially re-opened by the Duchess of Kent on May 1st, 1973.

When you look at the stations or the engines you may care to spare a thought for those whose foresight makes your journey possible: from Stephenson and his hardy navvies through to the volunteers of the past 30 years.

There is even a chance for you to play a part in the continuing railway story: as volunteer or shareholder. Ask at any station for details of how you can become involved with the North Yorkshire Moors Railway. You will then be helping preserve one of Britain's finest railways for our children and our children's children.

SO YOU WANT TO BE AN ENGINE DRIVER?

HOW THE LOCOMOTIVE WORKS

Over the years hundreds of different types of steam locos have been devised, but they all work in a similar way.

Fuel (usually coal, but sometimes wood or oil) is burnt on a **grate** at the bottom of a **firebox.** Flames and hot gases are drawn from the firebox through a series of parallel **tubes** in the **boiler** into the **smoke box** at the front of the loco.

Heat from the boiler tubes turns water in the boiler into steam which collects in the **steam dome** and then passes into the **cylinders** via a **regulator.**

The pressure of steam in the cylinder pushes a piston which in turn forces the connecting rod and crank to turn the driving axle of the wheels.

The exhaust steam escapes via a **blast pipe** into the **chimney** and at the same time draws more hot gases from the firebox through the boiler tubes.

THE MAIN FITTINGS ON THE ENGINE CAB

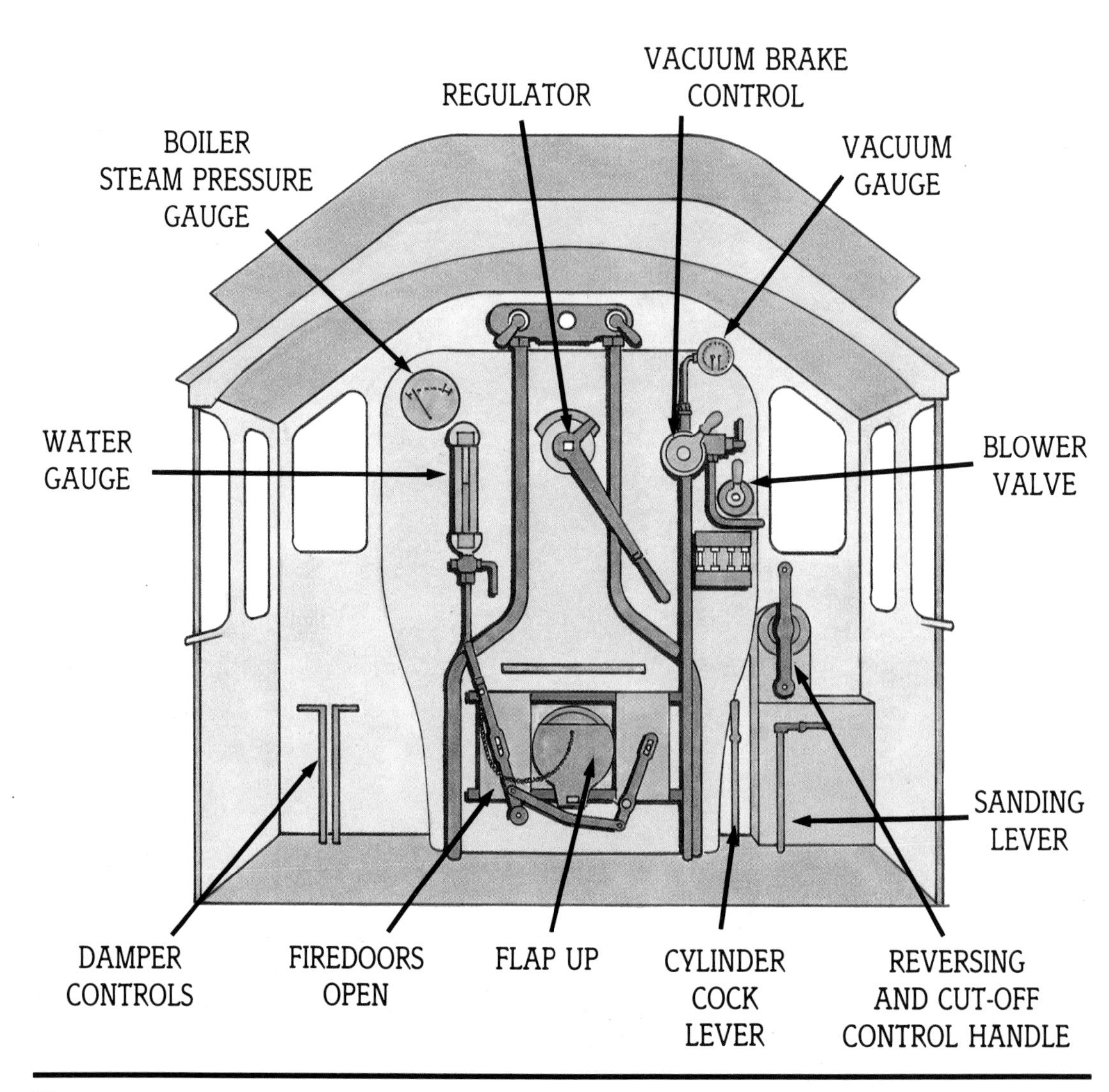

The main control is the **regulator.** This controls the flow of steam passing from the steam dome to the cylinder: more steam and the engine goes faster; less steam and it goes slower.
A safety valve in the steam dome automatically releases steam if the pressure gets too high.
The steam can also be used to power other things such as the loco's brakes, vacuum brakes on the train, heating and the whistle. Other controls in the cab enable the driver to select forward and reverse running, or more economical working at speed. There may be controls for the steam injector which maintains the water level in the boiler, whilst the blower helps to draw the fire when the engine is standing. There are several water and steam pressure gauges and of course, the whistle.

Sounds pretty easy doesn't it?

But just ask the driver!

WALKS AND TRAILS

The railway passes through some of the country's finest scenery and there are some superb walks from each station.

WAYMARK WALKS

Easy-to-follow leaflets showing a family walk from the station.
Pickering-Blandsby Park (Waymark 11)
Grosmont-Lease Rigg (Waymark 12)
Grosmont-Green End (Waymark 13)
Goathland-Darnholm and Water Ark (Waymark 14)
Goathland-Mallyan Spout and Beck Hole (Waymark 15)
Goathland-Roman Road (Waymark 26)

NEWTONDALE FOREST WALKS

A series of walks from Newtondale Halt.

HISTORICAL RAIL TRAIL

An easy walk following the original route of Stephenson's 1836 railway from Goathland to Grosmont.